USING FAVORITE PICTURE BOOKS

TO STIMULATE DISCUSSION AND ENCOURAGE CRITICAL THINKING

by Imogene Forte & Sandra Schurr

Incentive Publications, Inc.
Nashville, Tennessee

Illustrated by Marta Drayton
Cover by Becky Rüegger
Edited by Leslie Britt and Karla Westerman

ISBN 0-86530-314-2

PRINTED IN THE UNITED STATES OF AMERICA

TABLE OF CONTENTS

PREFACE

What were some of your best-loved picture books as a child? More than likely, you can recall not only the exact titles, but you can probably recite specific character names and even whole passages, explain the important events, and describe the types of illustrations in each book. Unfortunately, you may also be able to trace back to a time in your school history, somewhere around the fourth or fifth grade, when your teachers no longer shared or discussed these wonderful works of literature in class, and instead required mostly independent reading of textbooks or chapter books. As a student who had acquired the basic skills needed to read, your exposure to picture books had come to an unnecessary halt.

Educators today, in an effort to establish reasons why many intermediate and middle grade students lack both interest and insight in reading, seem to agree that all students benefit from opportunities to read and respond to a wide variety of literature. Yes, contrary to popular belief, older students *can* and *do* learn from picture books!

Using Favorite Picture Books To Stimulate Discussion and Encourage Critical Thinking presents a collection of lesson plans based on familiar children's picture books that have been assembled to promote a renewed love of reading, to stimulate students to share and discuss their opinions and ideas, and to encourage all to look again to uncover the meaning that is hidden between the lines or embedded within the pictures.

Organized in a clear, easy-to-follow format, each lesson is arranged in three sections. A brief synopsis gives teachers and students a general overview of the story's plot, setting, and characters. Carefully selected questions, listed as "Points To Ponder," encourage individual thought and stimulate class discussion. These questions may be used during and after reading to help students make the jump from a simple, literal interpretation to a higher, more sophisticated level of examination. Students are challenged to make predictions, draw conclusions, compare and contrast story elements, analyze character behaviors, and justify their opinions with reasons and explanations. The final section, "Projects To Pursue," provides many opportunities for extending the story and for bringing valuable personal meaning to what has been read and shared. By relating the picture book events to their own experiences and backgrounds, students discover the true importance of reading.

The fundamental concept underlying this comprehensive resource is a simple yet important one. If a picture is worth a thousand words, then, certainly, a book filled with many pictures should be considered priceless for students of all ages!

BOOK TITLE: *Alexander And The Terrible, Horrible, No Good, Very Bad Day*

AUTHOR: Judith Viorst
ILLUSTRATOR: Ray Cruz
PUBLISHER: Atheneum

SYNOPSIS:

For Alexander, this was a "terrible, horrible, no good, very bad day." From the time he woke up in the morning with gum in his hair to the time he sat down for dinner only to find lima beans on his plate and kissing on TV, Alexander couldn't seem to do anything right.

POINTS TO PONDER:

1. From your own experience, and after reading this story, write a definition to explain what a terrible, horrible, no good, very bad day is like. Now write a definition of a terrific, wonderful, totally awesome, very great day.

2. Do you think Alexander overreacted to the day's events? Why or why not?

3. How might you comfort Alexander if you were his teacher, mother, father, or sibling?

4. Do the illustrations enhance the message of the story? If so, how?

5. How would you describe Alexander's personality to your best friend?

PROJECTS TO PURSUE:

1. Write a journal account of your own terrible, horrible, no good, very bad day, either real or imaginary.

2. Pretend you are Alexander. Use expression and inflection to retell the story to your classmates as you feel the author intended him to sound.

3. Create a story like *Alexander and the Terrible, Horrible, No Good, Very Bad Day* without words. Draw a series of illustrations showing all types of problematic situations for a young girl or boy. Put them together in booklet form and have others supply the words as they flip through the drawings.

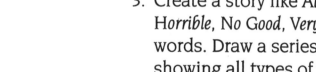

BOOK TITLE: The Alphabet From Z To A
(With Much Confusion On The Way)

AUTHOR: Judith Viorst
ILLUSTRATOR: Richard Hull
PUBLISHER: Atheneum

SYNOPSIS:

In this book, Judith Viorst explores the alphabet backwards, using this unorthodox approach to show how the spellings and sounds of our language are often inconsistent and confusing.

POINTS TO PONDER:

1. What impression are you left with after reading this book? Do you think this is how Judith Viorst wants you to feel?

2. What "quirks and quagmires" of the English language are portrayed in this story?

3. How do Richard Hull's drawings enrich the text of this book?

4. Would a person learning the English language find the information in this book useful or confusing? Defend your answer.

5. What do you think motivated Judith Viorst to write this book?

PROJECTS TO PURSUE:

1. Do some research to uncover other confusing spellings and sounds of our language that would frustrate students learning to write, read, and speak in English.

2. Use this book to create a choral reading activity for selected members of your class.

3. Choose one of your examples of confusing spellings and sounds from Project 1 and illustrate it in a style similar to that of Richard Hull.

**B**OOK TITLE: *Amazing Grace*

AUTHOR: Mary Hoffman
ILLUSTRATOR: Caroline Binch
PUBLISHER: Dial Books for Young Readers

**S**YNOPSIS:

Grace loves stories. She especially loves to act out the most exciting parts. She would pretend to be Joan of Arc, Anansi, and Hiawatha. At school, she wants to be Peter Pan, even though she is a girl and black. Grace's Nana helps her discover that she can be anything she wants if she puts her mind to it.

POINTS TO PONDER:

1. Why do you think Grace liked stories so much? Why did she like to act out parts of stories? How are you like Grace? In what ways are you different from her?

2. What might Grace do when she grows up?

3. Have you ever been told that you couldn't do something because of your age, sex, size, or race? What was your reaction?

4. What message is being conveyed by the author of this story? Is this message an important one for readers of all ages?

5. Describe the expressions and emotions illustrated in the pictures of this book.

6. Why is support by family members important to all of us?

PROJECTS TO PURSUE:

1. Make a list of favorite story characters. Take turns acting out characters to see if teammates can guess your choice. Define special actions you could make or words you could use to make your character easier to identify.

2. Read a version of Peter Pan. Choose a character from the story to describe in pictures or words.

3. Review a listing of current movies or TV shows. Discuss the main characters involved. How would a character from one show get along with a character from a different show? Make cartoon strips to illustrate your character interactions.

OOK TITLE: *Arithmetic*

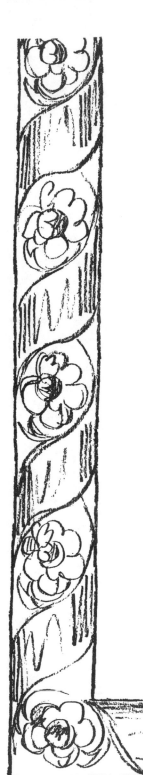

AUTHOR: Carl Sandburg
ILLUSTRATOR: Ted Rand
PUBLISHER: Harcourt Brace Jovanovich

YNOPSIS:

Based on the poem "Arithmetic" by Carl Sandburg, this book offers readers new ways of looking at the world from a mathematical perspective. Illustrator Ted Rand takes Sandburg's famous words and transforms them into a unique anamorphic adventure.

POINTS TO PONDER:

1. What does this book tell us about the language of numbers and arithmetic?

2. How would you define the concept of an "anamorphic image" and how does the illustrator incorporate it in his work?

3. Why might many readers identify with the messages in the poem by Carl Sandburg?

4. How does this book appeal to visual, auditory, and tactile learners?

5. What makes arithmetic so hard for some students and so easy for others?

PROJECTS TO PURSUE:

1. Read several other poems by Carl Sandburg and choose one of them to illustrate in a book similar to this one.

2. Try reading this book aloud and having a small group of peers act out the words in a dramatic mime.

3. Create a series of cartoon figures for each of the numerals one through nine. Use these to design a comic strip about arithmetic.

4. Make up a dance that explains arithmetic.

BOOK TITLE: *Beethoven Lives Upstairs*

AUTHOR: Barbara Nichol
ILLUSTRATOR: Scott Cameron
PUBLISHER: Orchard Books

SYNOPSIS:

This book weaves true incidents from Beethoven's life into a fictional correspondence between a young boy, Christoph, and his uncle, a music student in Salzburg. Christoph is upset with his mother who has taken a new tenant named Ludwig van Beethoven in their upstairs flat. Initially, Christoph dislikes the eccentric Mr. Beethoven, but over the course of his correspondence with his uncle, he develops a compassion for this famous composer.

POINTS TO PONDER:

1. Who was Ludwig van Beethoven? What was he like as a person?

2. Explain why Christoph began one of his early letters to his uncle with these words: "Something terrible has happened. A madman has moved into our house."

3. How would you describe Christoph at this period in his life, and why do you think he began writing to his Uncle Karl even though they did not know each other very well?

4. How did Christoph's attitude change toward Beethoven over time? Give specific examples from the story.

5. Do you think this story supports the idea that a book shouldn't be judged by its cover? Explain your answer.

PROJECTS TO PURSUE:

1. Bring a recording of Beethoven's music to school and play it for the class. Write a short essay describing its mood and its impact on you, the listener.

2. Stage a discussion or debate to examine the premise that many geniuses, like Beethoven, are also often mad and tormented as creative individuals.

3. Compose a letter that Christoph might have sent to Beethoven during the autumn of 1822 and a response that Beethoven might have sent to Christoph. What would they have said to one another?

4. Find out as much as you can about Beethoven's life. Make a time line showing important events. Write a journal entry that he might have written during one important period of his life.

BOOK TITLE:

A Chair For My Mother

AUTHOR: Vera B. Williams

ILLUSTRATOR: Vera B. Williams

PUBLISHER: Greenwillow Books

 ## SYNOPSIS:

Three generations of women work and struggle to replace their possessions that were destroyed in a fire. The story is told from the viewpoint of a young girl. She and her family work together to save enough money to purchase a new stuffed chair. The chair symbolizes more than just a piece of furniture.

POINTS TO PONDER:

1. Write and share a one-sentence summary that restates the primary message of the story. What one word best describes the story's theme? Explain why you picked this word.

2. How would it feel to lose all of your family's possessions in a fire? What item in your home would you probably miss the most? Why?

3. The overall mood of this story is positive. Explain how this is possible when the topic is such a tragic one.

4. Why do you think the author tells the story through the eyes of a young girl? How does this affect the story?

5. The writer uses symbolism to let the reader know that this family has lost more than furniture in the fire. Give some examples and tell how they are important.

PROJECTS TO PURSUE:

1. Think back to your school's last fire drill. Recall some behaviors by students that were disruptive or possibly even dangerous to themselves and others. Brainstorm with classmates a list of suggestions for improving these problems during the next fire drill. Design posters with catchy slogans of your ideas to display around campus as reminders of the importance of fire safety procedures.

2. Conduct a school-wide survey on attitudes about fire drills. A good question might be, "Do you take school fire drills seriously?" Poll a variety of people such as students, teachers, parents, principals, etc. Organize the information by creating a bar or pie graph. Discuss the results in small groups, trying to establish some conclusions about the attitudes of your school. You may wish to conduct the survey another time during the school year for comparison purposes, possibly after completing Project #1.

3. Research the number of homes destroyed by fire in the United States each year (visit the library, interview firefighters or fire victims, etc.). Write a television or radio announcement that includes these statistics. Offer listeners a few suggestions as to what could be done to reduce this number.

4. Rewrite parts of the story from another character's viewpoint. Share and discuss.

BOOK TITLE: *Cinder-Elly*

AUTHOR:	Frances Minters
ILLUSTRATOR:	G. Brian Karas
PUBLISHER:	Viking

SYNOPSIS:

This is a modern-day version of the Cinderella fairy tale written with a rhyming pattern. The story has an urban setting, giving the plot a new twist.

POINTS TO PONDER:

1. What makes this story amusing and interesting to read?

2. Who is Prince Charming in this story and how does he behave?

3. How does the godmother assist Elly with her problem?

4. What elements of the story make it modern?

5. How would you describe the artistic style of the illustrator G. Brian Karas?

PROJECTS TO PURSUE:

1. Construct a Venn diagram to compare and contrast the story elements of *Cinder-Elly* with a traditional version of the Cinderella story.

2. Work with a group of peers to use this book as the basis for performing a choral reading or skit for a group of younger students.

3. Choose another popular fairy tale such as *Little Red Riding Hood* or *Goldilocks and the Three Bears* and rewrite it with a modern twist.

4. Write a script for a video presentation of *Cinder-Elly*. List the visuals necessary for the production of your script.

BOOK TITLE: *Cloudy With A Chance Of Meatballs*

AUTHOR: Judi Barrett
ILLUSTRATOR: Ron Barrett
PUBLISHER: Atheneum

SYNOPSIS:

In this story, the reader learns what life would be like if food dropped like rain from the sky. The people who live in the community of Chewandswallow are happy when the weather serves food they like to eat; however, when the weather turns bad, they encounter all types of problems.

POINTS TO PONDER:

1. Could this story be classified as a parody and/or a tall tale? Give examples to support your answer.

2. Why do you think the author chose to name the town Chewandswallow? What might be some other appropriate names for the town in keeping with the story's theme?

3. Would you like to live in a community like Chewandswallow? Why or why not?

4. How would you describe the illustrations in this book?

5. Think about some of the problems encountered by the people in Chewandswallow and how they handled them. Explain how you might have solved some of the problems differently.

PROJECTS TO PURSUE:

1. Pretend you are the weatherman for the community of Chewandswallow. Prepare a weather report for one week that would make the people of the town very happy. Draw a series of illustrations to portray each day's menu.

2. Create a map of your own make-believe community.

3. Create a menu of foods that make you happy. Include items for breakfast, lunch, dinner, and snacks. Remember to include some mouth-watering illustrations.

4. Think of some other titles for this story that use weather-related terminology, phrases, or jargon.

BOOK TITLE: *A Color Of His Own*

AUTHOR: Leo Lionni
ILLUSTRATOR: Leo Lionni
PUBLISHER: Pantheon Books

SYNOPSIS:

A little chameleon is sad upon discovering that his color changes when he changes locations. He becomes determined to find a color of his own. As he searches for his identity, he meets an older and wiser chameleon who shows him that change is not always so bad.

POINTS TO PONDER:

1. Why is the chameleon so unhappy with his ability to blend into his surroundings?

2. Are the illustrations important to the story? Why or why not?

3. Is it reassuring to identify others who have characteristics similar to our own? Explain your answer.

4. What does this fable teach us about nature?

5. Does this fable have a connection to your everyday life in school?

PROJECTS TO PURSUE:

1. Experiment with paint to see how the colors blend with one another and change each other. Water-based paint will work best for this activity. Combine your efforts to make a class mural or collage.

2. Research to find information on chameleons. Why do they take on the colors of their surroundings? Where do they live? What do they eat?

3. Examine other changes in nature by watching plants grow in the classroom. Lentils sprout quickly in a shallow pan of water. Carrot tops, sweet potatoes, avocado seeds, and a pineapple top are food items that will quickly turn into plants on the classroom windowsill.

4. Count how many color changes are illustrated in the book. Compile a list of objects upon which the chameleon could be sitting to become the different colors.

BOOK TITLE: *Dear Mr. Blueberry*

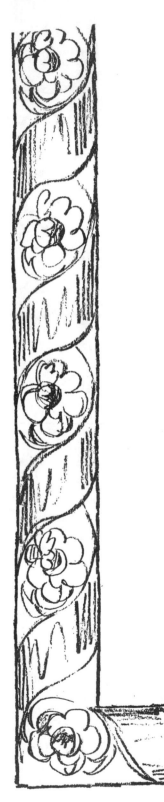

AUTHOR: Simon James
ILLUSTRATOR: Simon James
PUBLISHER: Macmillan

SYNOPSIS:

Emily writes a series of letters to her teacher, Mr. Blueberry, telling him that a whale lives in her pond. She asks him for more information about these creatures. Mr. Blueberry responds by giving Emily information about whales in each letter while trying to convince her that whales are migratory and can't live in ponds.

POINTS TO PONDER:

1. Why is Emily convinced that a whale lives in her pond?

2. How does Mr. Blueberry respond to Emily's letters?

3. What facts did you learn about whales in this story?

4. How would you describe Emily as a person and as a personality?

5. Have you ever written a letter to one of your teachers? Would you ever? Explain your response.

PROJECTS TO PURSUE:

1. Design and write a thank-you note from Emily to Mr. Blueberry. Include some facts about whales so that he knows he actually helped you.

2. Read to find out more about whales. Use the format of this story to create a series of additional letters between Emily and Mr. Blueberry that discuss the habits and habitats of whales.

3. Write an "Ode to the Whale." Read about odes so that you write your poem in the correct style.

4. Plan a perfect vacation for you and a friend at the beach near a place for whale watching. Where might you be able to do this, and what would you do on your trip?

5. Compose a book like *Dear Mr. Blueberry* about another animal of special interest to you.

BOOK TITLE:

Dinner At Aunt Connie's House

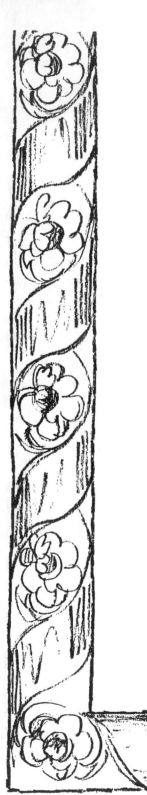

AUTHOR: Faith Ringgold
ILLUSTRATOR: Faith Ringgold
PUBLISHER: Hyperion Books for Children

SYNOPSIS:

This is a powerful story about how two young children, Melody and Lonnie, discover their heritage through twelve beautiful portraits of famous African-American women painted by their Aunt Connie, an artist.

POINTS TO PONDER:

1. How do Aunt Connie's family members react to her dinner surprises? Is this the reaction she had hoped to get? What leads you to believe this?

2. What similarities do you see among the twelve African-American women that Aunt Connie chose to paint?

3. How do the illustrations tie the story together and emphasize the author's message?

4. What do you think is meant by the African proverb: "A good tree grows among thorns"? How does it relate to the story?

PROJECTS TO PURSUE:

1. Rewrite this book by selecting twelve famous African-American men for portraits in the attic. Who would they be and what would you say to them?

2. Research to find other examples of African proverbs. Write them down and relate them to personal experiences that you and others in your class have had. Write a journal entry for each one.

3. Read to find more information about other popular minority artists. Produce a one-page picture essay of their lives and artistic contributions.

4. Do some research to find out who the author, Faith Ringgold, is and where she got her ideas for this book. Write a mini-biography of her life.

BOOK TITLE: *Earrings!*

AUTHOR: Judith Viorst
ILLUSTRATOR: Nola Langner Malone
PUBLISHER: Atheneum

SYNOPSIS:

In this story, a young girl uses a variety of persuasive techniques to convince her parents to let her have pierced ears.

POINTS TO PONDER:

1. What arguments does the girl use to try to convince her parents to let her get her ears pierced? In your opinion, which of these arguments makes the most sense or is most worthy? Why?

2. Why do some people want pierced ears?

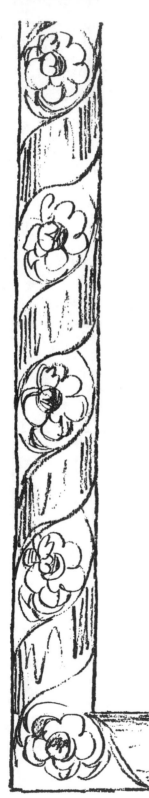

3. Why do you think Judith Viorst is such a popular author with young people today?

4. What methods have you used to get your parents to behave in a certain way? How successful were they?

5. How would you describe the physical appearance and personality of the girl in this story?

PROJECTS TO PURSUE:

1. Using magic markers, crayons, or colored pencils, design a pair of pierced earrings that you would like to have.

2. Role play a scenario between the girl and her parents in which she pleads to have her ears pierced.

3. Write a set of 10 "I would, if only . . ." statements about you and your parents, following this model:
   "I *would clean my room every week if only my parents would let me decorate it the way I want to.*"

4. Design a book jacket and write ad copy for this book that would make it attractive to a potential buyer.

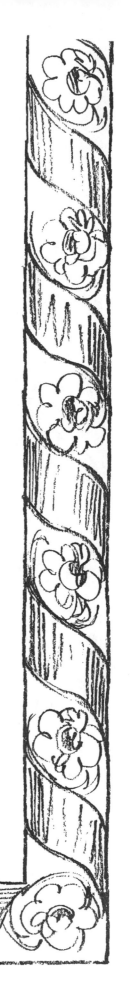

BOOK TITLE:

The Fall Of
Freddie The Leaf

AUTHOR: Leo Buscaglia
ILLUSTRATOR: Leo Buscaglia
PUBLISHER: Charles B. Slack

SYNOPSIS:

This is a simple story about a leaf named Freddie. How Freddie and his companion leaves change with the passing season makes a warm allegory illustrating the delicate balance between life and death.

POINTS TO PONDER:

1. What is an allegory? How is it used in this story?

2. Which season of the year is your favorite and why?

3. What does Freddie learn from Daniel?

4. Do you think the use of photographs to illustrate the ideas in this story is effective? Give reasons for your answer.

5. What other lessons about life might we learn from nature?

PROJECTS TO PURSUE:

1. Take photographs of trees in a variety of settings. Mount your photographs in a photo album and write a caption for each one.

2. Research to find out more scientific facts about the seasons and their influence on nature. Make a diagram showing how one of these changes works or functions.

3. Use a leaf print design to create an unusual wallpaper, wrapping paper, or stationery motif.

4. Compose an ode to a leaf. Read about odes to make sure you write yours in the correct style.

BOOK TITLE: Fathers, Mothers, Sisters, Brothers

AUTHOR: Mary Ann Hoberman

ILLUSTRATOR: Marylin Hafner

PUBLISHER: Joy Street Books

SYNOPSIS:

This is a collection of family poems. There are poems about grandparents, baby-sitters, extended families, divorced families, and adoptive families. The poems are wise, witty, insightful, and lots of fun to read.

POINTS TO PONDER:

1. Does this book of poems reflect today's changing definition of family? Explain your answer.

2. Which poem is your favorite? Why?

3. Which of the poems seems to best represent you and your family situation? Give reasons for your answer.

4. Find examples from the book to show that the poems written by Mary Ann Hoberman are "witty, wise, and insightful." Be specific in your comments.

5. How would you describe the artwork created by illustrator Marilyn Hafner?

PROJECTS TO PURSUE:

1. Work with a group of peers and have each person select a poem to memorize. Practice reciting them aloud and videotape your final delivery. Add an introduction and an explanation to the video tape. Make it available in the school media center for check-out in the poetry section.

2. Locate another poem by a different author on the topic of fathers, mothers, sisters, or brothers. Compare and contrast this poem with one from Hoberman's book. How are they alike and how are they different?

3. Write an original poem about families.

BOOK TITLE: *The Giving Tree*

AUTHOR: Shel Silverstein
ILLUSTRATOR: Shel Silverstein
PUBLISHER: Harper & Row

SYNOPSIS:

In this story, a young boy befriends a tree. As he grows up, the boy wants more and more from the tree, and the tree continues to give. Silverstein's parable offers a moving interpretation of the gift of giving and the capacity to give in return.

POINTS TO PONDER:

1. What is the significance of this story's title?

2. This story is considered to be a parable. What message is the author trying to convey?

3. How does this book represent "sadness, along with consolation"?

4. What special feeling do the graphics convey?

5. Do you ever find solace in, or peace from, nature? Explain.

6. Who is the most giving person you know? Defend your answer with examples.

PROJECTS TO PURSUE:

1. Role play a variety of incidents with the message: "It's better to give than to receive."

2. Research to find out how scientists and mathematicians calculate to find out the age of a tree. Create an appendix page for the book *The Giving Tree* by writing your information and illustrating it with a drawing or diagram.

3. Pretend you are the giving tree. Create a diary and write an entry following each of the boy's visits. Try to capture the thoughts and feelings of the tree.

BOOK TITLE: The Guy Who Was Five Minutes Late

AUTHOR: William G. Grossman
ILLUSTRATOR: Judy Glasser
PUBLISHER: Harper & Row

SYNOPSIS:

From the day he was born, this guy has always been five minutes late. All ends happily, however, after he meets and marries a princess who is always late for the important events in her life.

POINTS TO PONDER:

1. What are some consequences of being late for important events in your life?

2. What suggestions can you think of that might help this boy learn to be on time?

3. What do you think is the author's purpose for writing this story?

4. Do you have a friend or acquaintance who is often late for appointments with you? What are the effects of his or her tardiness on your relationship?

5. What would be the consequence of the following scenarios?
   - A heart surgeon shows up late for emergency surgery.
   - A middle-grade teacher is five minutes late for every class period.
   - A groom appears late for his own wedding.
   - A seventh-grade student is consistently late in turning in her homework.

PROJECTS TO PURSUE:

1. Rewrite the story of *The Guy Who Was Five Minutes Late* so that he was early for every event in his life.

2. Analyze your own schedule for the past week. Were you late for some events? Would you say your friends and family consider you to be a person who is usually on time, often not on time, or always late?

3. Make up a story about a magic clock that ensures its owner against being late for any appointment.

4. Use a thesaurus and/or a dictionary to make a list of as many words as you can think of that mean the same (or almost the same) as "late" and as many words as you can think of that mean the opposite. Design a crossword or word find puzzle using your words.

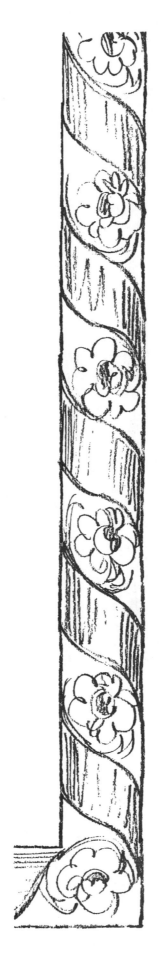

BOOK TITLE:

Hailstones And Halibut Bones

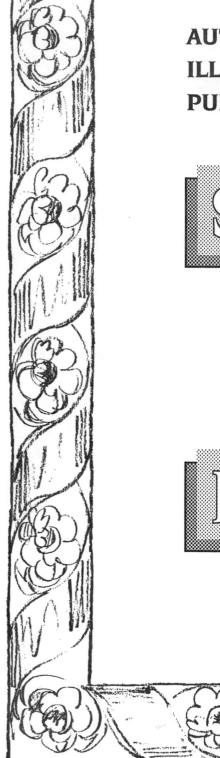

AUTHOR: Mary O'Neill
ILLUSTRATOR: John Wallner
PUBLISHER: Doubleday

SYNOPSIS:

Hailstones and Halibut Bones is a book of poetry which focuses on the colors of the spectrum. It has become a modern children's classic. The book is lavishly illustrated, and its poetry is a commentary on the feelings and meanings of colors.

POINTS TO PONDER:

1. What is the significance of the book's title?

2. In what ways does the author portray the different colors for the reader?

3. Which color poem is your favorite and why?

4. Does the author appeal to the five senses in each of her poems? Give examples to support your answer.

5. How do the illustrations reflect the theme of each poem?

PROJECTS TO PURSUE:

1. Write a color poem using Mary O'Neill's language pattern for a hue of your choice not included in the book. Consider such possibilities as magenta, chartreuse, turquoise, lavender, or jade.

2. Make a color scrapbook using your own creative artwork. Write descriptions for each page using color words and colorful metaphors when possible.

3. Design a greeting card that incorporates a box of crayons in its illustration and a color pun in its message.

Example: Happy Birthday! Hope your day brings you fun in every color!

BOOK TITLE: *Hey, Al*

AUTHOR: Arthur Yorinks
ILLUSTRATOR: Richard Egielski
PUBLISHER: Farrar, Straus, Giroux

SYNOPSIS:

A mysterious bird appears to transport Al, a janitor, and his dog, Eddie, on a magical journey. New worlds await as they travel from their modest apartment to an island paradise in the sky. After several misadventures, Al and Eddie decide that "be it ever so humble, home is after all the best place to be."

POINTS TO PONDER:

1. Where would you want to go if a magic bird appeared to provide you with the same opportunity provided for Al and Eddie?

2. How well do you think the illustrations by Richard Egielski interpret Al's character and personality?

3. Do you think the story would have been as interesting without Eddie as a main character? Explain your answer.

4. How do you think this experience will influence Al's future life?

PROJECTS TO PURSUE:

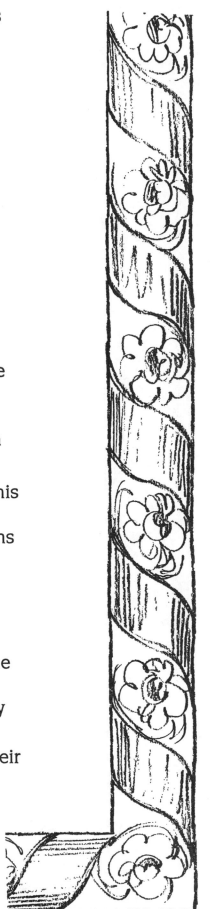

1. Draw or paint a picture of an animal you would substitute for the bird in the story. Tell why you visualized this particular animal.

2. Al's experiences on the exotic island in the sky caused him to appreciate the positive aspects of his home. Make a list of ten things you would miss if you left your own home.

3. Al's dog, Eddie, was an important part of his life. Select one of these statements with which to agree or disagree and give reasons for your position.

   • People who have pets live happier and fuller lives than people who do not.

   • Every kid should have a pet.

   • Pets are a big responsibility, and no one should consider owning a pet without considering the commitment necessary for its care.

   • Pets are a nuisance and a bother for their owners and other people in the neighborhood.

4. Design a cartoon based on one of these expressions.
   "It's a dog's life."
   "the dog days of summer"
   "in the dog house"

BOOK TITLE:

A House For Hermit Crab

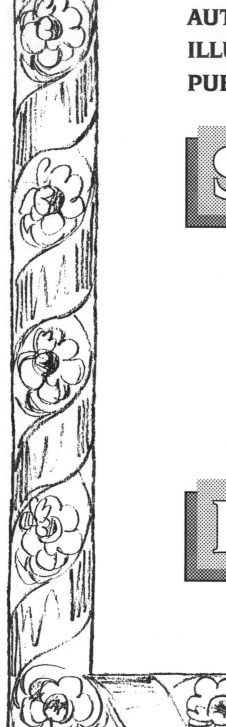

AUTHOR: Eric Carle
ILLUSTRATOR: Eric Carle
PUBLISHER: Picture Book Studio

SYNOPSIS:

One January, Hermit Crab outgrows his snug shell house. He moves into a larger shell which feels good, but is too plain. He finds beautiful and useful undersea creatures with which to decorate and enhance his new home. By November, Hermit Crab again decides his new house is too small. Although sad about leaving his friends and familiar house, he searches for a new, larger shell. A year had passed and Hermit Crab had grown, not only in size but in confidence as well.

POINTS TO PONDER:

1. Have there been times in your life when you felt afraid to try something new? Explain your answer.

2. Discuss why Hermit Crab was not as afraid to search for a new home the second time.

3. In what ways are Hermit Crab's sea creature neighbors like family?

4. Why are the simple collage-type line drawings so effective in this book?

5. Why do you think Eric Carle chose to include information about hermit crabs in the front of this book as well as a glossary of the sea creatures in the back? How is this information useful to the reader?

PROJECTS TO PURSUE:

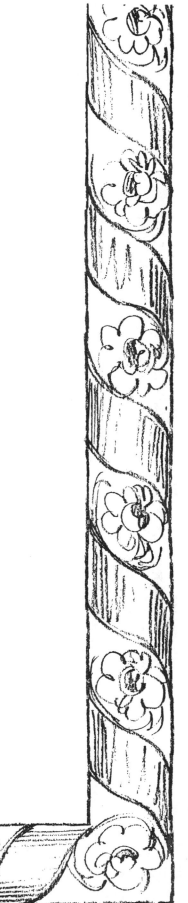

1. Research hermit crabs and list facts about their existence. Where do they live? Whose shells do they borrow for houses? What do they eat? Share your list and then compare it to lists made by researching sea anemones, starfish, corals, snails, sea urchins, and lantern fish.

2. Create an underwater scene in a large cardboard box or on a bulletin board. Make hermit crabs of various sizes and decorate their shell houses with all kinds of undersea creatures. Use as many different kinds of art materials as possible.

3. Make a mosaic hermit crab shell house from cardboard, clay, or papier mâché and cover it with real shell pieces. (If shells are unavailable, use noodles and macaroni.)

4. Develop a time line to show the life cycle of a hermit crab.

5. Write a letter to a real-estate agent pretending you are a hermit crab. In the letter, describe what your perfect home (shell) would be like.

BOOK TITLE:

A House Is A House For Me

AUTHOR: Mary Ann Hoberman
ILLUSTRATOR: Betty Fraser
PUBLISHER: Viking Press

SYNOPSIS:

The book uses words and detailed illustrations of a variety of homes, people, body parts, and even thoughts to extend the definition of a house. For example, a mirror is shown to be a house for reflections, a book is a house for a story, and a rose is a house for a smell.

POINTS TO PONDER:

1. According to the story, "It seems that whatever you see is either a house or it lives in a house . . ." What do you think the writer means by this statement?

2. Does every creature have a house of its own? Explain.

3. On the last five pages of the book, the illustrations are quite detailed and there is very little text. Discuss the impact of this creative publishing decision.

4. Who is the narrator of the story?

5. What are the possibilities for a house for you?

PROJECTS TO PURSUE:

1. List as many animals as can be named in a ten-minute period. After the list is made, identify possible houses for each animal. Use reference materials as necessary. Who can share houses?

2. Research the building of a house. Identify the materials needed to build a house as well as the professionals needed to get the job done.

3. Books are houses for stories. Report on a favorite story. Give your story a framework, telling the who, what, when, and where. Then build the story by describing what happens to the characters. Finish your "story house" by summarizing in two or three sentences the ending of the story, moral, or main point the author tried to make as you see it. Illustrate your story in "house" format—from foundation to roof.

BOOK TITLE: *I Hate To Read*

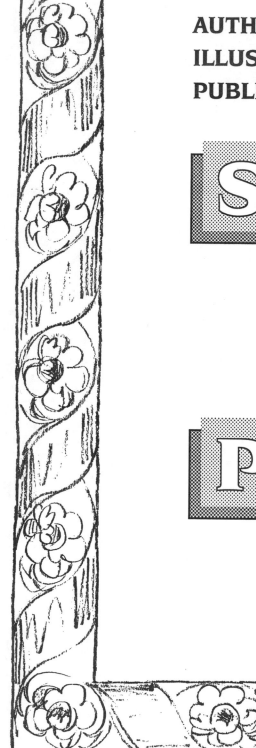

AUTHOR: Rita Marshall
ILLUSTRATOR: Etienne Delessert
PUBLISHER: Creative Education

SYNOPSIS:

Victor Dickens hates to read, or at least he thinks he does. While pretending to read, he discovers a crocodile who introduces him to a new set of friends. Because of his adventure in words, Victor decides that reading might not be such a bad thing after all.

POINTS TO PONDER:

1. Why do you think Victor Dickens and his friends hate to read?

2. What happens to change Victor's mind about reading? Can you remember when you first discovered a book you liked and could read for yourself?

3. What is your favorite childhood book, and who is your favorite character? Why?

4. What would you say to a younger student who thinks he or she doesn't like to read?

5. Explain how the illustrations in this book help to create an excitement for reading.

6. Would you want to read about the characters in Victor's book? Why or why not?

PROJECTS TO PURSUE:

1. Conduct a class survey to determine the top three favorite picture books among students in your class. In groups, design a graph, chart, and other pictorial representation to show this information in a variety of forms.

2. Choose one of your favorite picture book characters. Create a name poem to describe this character. Write and illustrate your poem on a large piece of paper. Hang it up on a wall to display.

3. Share favorite picture books with a younger student. Use expression in your reading and talk about the characters and adventures in the story. This could be done as a class project.

4. Record picture book stories on tape so that younger non-reading students can share in the joy of stories.

BOOK TITLE: *I Want To Be*

AUTHOR: Thylias Moss
ILLUSTRATOR: Jerry Pinkney
PUBLISHER: Dial Books for Young Readers

SYNOPSIS:

The distinguished poet Thylias Moss uses her gift of writing to encourage young readers to stretch their imaginations and to experience everything there is to know in our miraculous and astonishing universe. She hopes to help young readers answer the question: "What do you want to be?"

POINTS TO PONDER:

1. How does the author use the figurative language of poetry to tell her story?

2. What are some of the things that the main character of the story wants to be when she grows up?

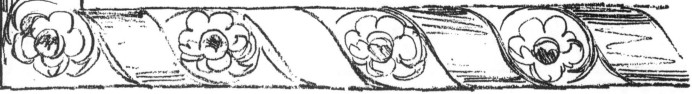

3. How would you describe the artwork of illustrator Jerry Pinkney?

4. How does Thylias Moss use the art of contradiction and opposites to make her point?

5. If you were to name the main character and identify the setting of this story, what would they be?

PROJECTS TO PURSUE:

1. Write a short monologue or personal essay to answer the question: "What do you want to be?"

2. Does a person always have a choice in what they want to be? Design a set of interview questions and survey a number of adults to address this issue.

3. Create an original drawing or picture that illustrates one of the metaphors from the story, such as: "I want to be a leaf that is part canoe riding the water as if it's a liquid horse."

4. Give this book a new title. Write a paragraph telling why you think yours is a fitting title.

 **OOK TITLE:** *I Was All Thumbs*

AUTHOR: Bernard Waber
ILLUSTRATOR: Bernard Waber
PUBLISHER: Houghton Mifflin

YNOPSIS:

This is a whimsical and engaging story about an octopus who has known only the quiet world of the laboratory and now is forced to venture out into the perils and pleasures of ocean life.

OINTS TO PONDER:

1. Who was Captain Pierre, and why did he release Legs into the sea?

2. Give some examples of puns from this story.

3. How would you describe the illustrations in this book?

4. What do you think is the author's primary message?

5. What is the significance of the book's title?

PROJECTS TO PURSUE:

1. Research the octopus and compile a list of facts about this unusual sea creature.

2. Assume the role of an underwater architect and create an unusual design for a city called Octopus-Metropolis.

3. Imagine you are a famous marine scientist like Captain Pierre. Compile a set of chapter titles for your award-winning book *A Day in the Life of an Octopus*.

BOOK TITLE: *If I Were A Penguin*

AUTHOR: Heidi Goennel
ILLUSTRATOR: Heidi Goennel
PUBLISHER: Little, Brown

SYNOPSIS:

This simple picture book explores what it would be like to be different kinds of animals from the perspective of a small child. After listing the positive aspects of several animals, the book concludes with the statement: "But mostly I'm happy to be just me."

POINTS TO PONDER:

1. If you could be any animal, which one would you choose to be? Why do you think you identify so strongly with this animal?

2. How would you talk about this book to a younger child? Is there a lesson you would try to explain? What is it?

3. Discuss other stories that describe why we should want to be ourselves.

4. The illustrations in this book are simple yet expressive. What techniques does the artist use to achieve this effect?

PROJECTS TO PURSUE:

1. Choose an animal not described in this book and list both positive and negative aspects of being that animal. Illustrate your answers.

2. Think about being yourself. Write about the reasons you like being you. What is one thing that you would like to change about yourself?

3. Make a list of things you like about a classmate. Share your feelings.

4. Research one of the animals described in the book. Report on its habitat, eating habits, life cycle, means of protection, and daily activities. Illustrate and display your findings.

My Friend Jessie
1. She is pretty
2. She is smart
3. She smiles a lot
4.

 **BOOK TITLE:**

 *If There Were Dreams To Sell*

AUTHOR: Compiled by Barbara Lalicki
ILLUSTRATOR: Margot Tomes
PUBLISHER: Lothrop, Lee, & Shepard

 **SYNOPSIS:**

This book contains a wide-ranging selection of quotes for each letter of the alphabet from sources as diverse as Mother Goose, John Donne, Emily Dickinson, and J.R.R. Tolkien.

 **POINTS TO PONDER:**

1. Which element appears to be more important in setting the tone of the book: the selection of the quotes or the artist's illustrations?

2. How do you think the author and the illustrator worked together to produce such an unusual work?

3. Does the wide range in levels of sophistication, word usage, and imagery enhance or detract from the book's effectiveness? Explain your conclusion.

4. Think of all of the people to whom you would like to give a book as a gift. Which of these people would you give *If There Were Dreams To Sell*? Do you see it as a more appropriate gift for an adult, a teenager, or a child? Would you like to receive this book as a gift?

PROJECTS TO PURSUE:

1. Think carefully about the title of the book. Think of another title that could have been used instead and design a book jacket with the new title.

2. Write a review of *If There Were Dreams To Sell* for a literary magazine or for the book page of your local newspaper.

3. Choose any one letter's selection and pantomime it for the class. Ask other class members to do the same and have fun guessing the letter selections being acted out.

4. Work with a cooperative learning group to compile selections for your own *If There Were Dreams To Sell* book. Illustrate each of your selections.

BOOK TITLE:

If You Made A Million

AUTHOR: David M. Schwartz
ILLUSTRATOR: Steven Kellogg
PUBLISHER: Lothrop, Lee, & Shepard

SYNOPSIS:

Marvelosissimo the Mathematical Magician helps the reader explore the fascinating world of money. He uses many tricks to show different ways that money can be spent, can be saved, and can grow.

POINTS TO PONDER:

1. How would you describe the writing style of the author?

2. What money concepts did you learn from this book?

3. How does the author combine reality and fantasy in the telling of his money tales?

4. Why are the illustrations considered to be an integral part of this book's message?

5. How could this book be used as a learning tool in the classroom?

PROJECTS TO PURSUE:

1. Write a short essay answering the question, "What would you do if you made a million dollars?"

2. Design a new set of United States currency. What bills and coins would you use and what would they look like?

3. Stage a classroom debate on the pros and cons of million-dollar lotteries in your state.

4. Create a mock lottery for your class. What rules and rewards will control your lottery process?

BOOK TITLE: *I'll Fix Anthony*

AUTHOR: Judith Viorst
ILLUSTRATOR: Arnold Lobel
PUBLISHER: Harper & Row

SYNOPSIS:

A younger brother dreams of being six years old and able to show that he is better than his older brother, Anthony. He thinks that Anthony doesn't care about him, even though his mother tells him that Anthony loves him.

POINTS TO PONDER:

1. Do you remember wanting to be six years old so that you could be big? Give examples.

2. Do you think Anthony loves his little brother? Why do you think he doesn't act like it?

3. If we did not have the illustrations in this book, would we know if the story was told by a little sister or little brother? Does the gender of the main character affect the story?

4. How would you "fix Anthony"?

5. What do you think is the hidden desire of the little brother? What does he want to know?

6. What age group would particularly enjoy this book?

7. Does the idea of planning for when you are older apply to your life now? If so, in what way?

PROJECTS TO PURSUE:

1. Illustrate a time when you have felt left out by a family member. Use either words, pictures, or a combination of both.

2. List things you can do to help younger family members feel more important. Do the same for what family members can do to make you feel more adult-like. Compare lists.

3. Use a cartoon format to illustrate a humorous event between two siblings.

4. Why is six such a big year in the process of growing up? Write about an incident that happened when you were six that made you feel more grown-up.

**B**OOK TITLE:

I'll See You In My Dreams

AUTHOR: Mavis Jukes
ILLUSTRATOR: Stacey Schuett
PUBLISHER: Alfred A. Knopf

SYNOPSIS:

This beautiful story of a young girl having to say good-bye to a loved one uses the metaphor of skywriting to convey the message of love to the reader.

POINTS TO PONDER:

1. Is the skywriting metaphor effective? Why or why not?

2. Who is ill and what is the prognosis for recovery? How do you know this?

3. How old is the main character of this story? What makes you think this?

4. What is a skywriter, and when are you likely to see one in the air?

5. What five words would you use to describe the illustrator's style? What period in art history would you say her work is most like? Explain.

PROJECTS TO PURSUE:

1. Create a simple picture book for very young children about airplanes. Use skywriting as the format for writing the text.

2. Design a series of paper airplanes and decorate them in various ways. Use them to conduct a paper airplane flying contest for the class.

3. Skywriting resembles clouds. Write a haiku about clouds, the sky, or what it feels like to fly in the sky.

BOOK TITLE: *Imagine*

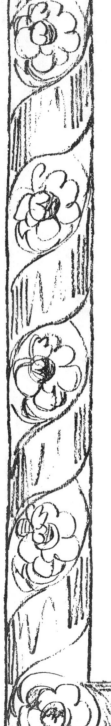

AUTHOR: Alison Lester
ILLUSTRATOR: Alison Lester
PUBLISHER: Houghton Mifflin

SYNOPSIS:

This book serves as a wonderful introduction to the animal world. The detailed pictures provide the reader with a perspective on many different habitats from around the world.

POINTS TO PONDER:

1. What is unusual about this picture book? Do you consider it a work of fiction or nonfiction?

2. Why might someone refer to this book as a "zoological treat"?

3. Which of the animal communities or habitats depicted is of most interest to you? Why?

4. How would you define imagination, and how does one go about imagining? How do you know when someone is imaginative? Is the ability to imagine a desirable trait?

5. How might this book be used as a teaching or learning tool?

PROJECTS TO PURSUE:

1. Choose one of the animal community settings in the book and research the animal life in that setting. Compile a fact book on the creatures suggested by the author.

2. Write another page for this book following the language pattern of:

    "Imagine if we were . . . ."
    Find someone to help you illustrate it.

3. Construct a diorama of one of the scenes in the book.

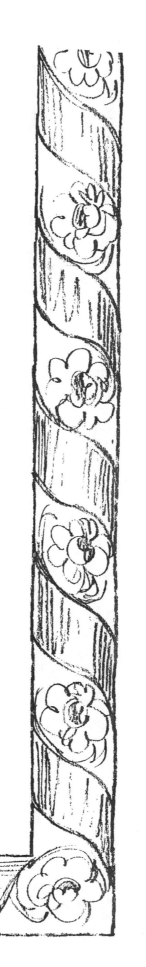

BOOK TITLE:

Leo
The Late Bloomer

AUTHOR: Robert Kraus
ILLUSTRATOR: Jose Aruego
PUBLISHER: Windmill Books

SYNOPSIS:

Leo is a tiger cub who doesn't seem to be learning and maturing as fast as he should. Leo's father is quite concerned about this "developmental lag," but Leo's mother urges patience and is confident that time will take care of their son's problem. And it does!

POINTS TO PONDER:

1. What does the word bloom mean in a scientific sense? How does this definition relate to Leo's situation?

2. How do Leo's mother and father differ in their concern for Leo's failure to grow and learn?

3. What is meant by the statement: "A watched bloomer doesn't bloom"?

4. What factors do you think accounted for Leo's maturation and subsequent statement: "I made it!"

5. Why are the illustrations important to the message of the story?

PROJECTS TO PURSUE:

1. Pretend that you have a friend who is a late bloomer. Write a letter to this person giving advice to make him or her feel better.

2. Write a simple oral history about a time when you had difficulty learning or doing something new.

3. Draw a series of pictures to show ways that you would like to bloom this year.

4. Create a cartoon to depict a humorous experience that Leo and his parents may have experienced.

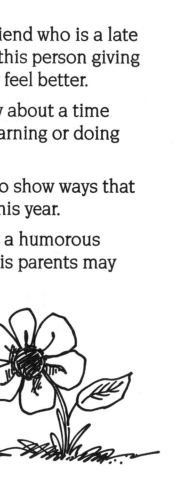

BOOK TITLE:

The Magic School Bus: Inside The Human Body

AUTHOR: Joanna Cole
ILLUSTRATOR: Bruce Degen
PUBLISHER: Scholastic

SYNOPSIS:

Ms. Frizzle again uses the Magic School Bus to take her students on an imaginative trip—this time through the human body, providing them with a close-up view of how human bodies get energy from food.

POINTS TO PONDER:

1. What words or phrases would you use to describe the mood or tone of this story?

2. Would you consider this book to be more like a textbook, a fairy tale, or a children's picture book? Give reasons for your answer.

3. What facts did you learn about the human body from this book?

4. How would you describe the format or page layout of this book? How does it work to convey the information in the book?

5. Why is this book likely to be appealing to students of every age?

6. Would you like to have Ms. Frizzle as a teacher? Why or why not?

 PROJECTS TO PURSUE:

1. Use this book as a model for writing about another adventure in the Magic School Bus. Consider a math-related topic, such as a trip inside a calculator, computer, cash register, or vending machine.

2. Compile an illustrated glossary of terms from the information presented in the book.

3. Try writing a thank-you note to Ms. Frizzle, letting her know how much you enjoyed the field trip and where you would like to go on the next one.

BOOK TITLES: *Many Luscious Lollipops* and *Merry-Go-Round*

AUTHOR: Ruth Heller
ILLUSTRATOR: Ruth Heller
PUBLISHER: Grosset & Dunlap

SYNOPSIS:

Furthering the student's grasp of the meaning and function of both adjectives and nouns, these two lovely picture books provide a rhymed text to increase one's understanding of hcw language looks and sounds.

POINTS TO PONDER:

1. How do these books enhance one's understanding of nouns and adjectives?

2. Why would these books be helpful to a teacher or student who wanted to learn more about the parts of speech?

3. Which are harder to use properly in your writing: adjectives or nouns? Explain your answer.

4. How would you describe the graphics in these books?

PROJECTS TO PURSUE:

1. Make a list of grammatical rules with examples that are presented in each of these books.

2. Use one of these books as the basis for a choral reading.

3. Use one of the books as a prototype for writing a similar book about verbs or adverbs.

4. Make a list of your ten favorite adjectives and/or your ten favorite nouns. Use one of these lists to write a paragraph about a topic of interest to people of your age using all of the ten words in some meaningful way.

BOOK TITLE:

May I Bring A Friend?

AUTHOR: Beatrice de Regniers
ILLUSTRATOR: Beni Montresor
PUBLISHER: Atheneum

SYNOPSIS:

An inventive boy turns an invitation to tea with the King and Queen into a delightful Sunday afternoon tea at the zoo. After permission is granted for the first friend to come along, the list of additional guests grows quickly. The party provides a happy turn of events for all concerned.

POINTS TO PONDER:

1. If you were invited to tea with the King and Queen and could bring only one other person, who would you bring? Why?

2. Do you think the King and Queen were happy with the way the tea party turned out?

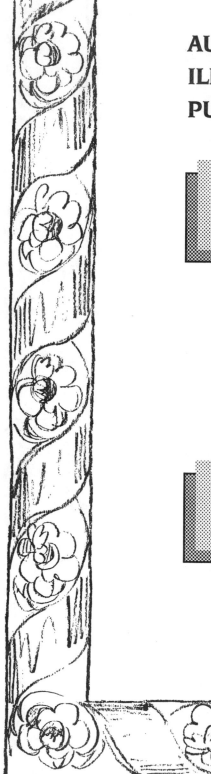

3. If you could have a tea party at the zoo, what kind of entertainment would you plan?

4. How do you think the illustrations contributed to the success of this book? Would you classify the illustrations as playful, serious, cartoon-like, or whimsical? Select the one word you think best describes the illustrator's style and explain your answer.

 PROJECTS TO PURSUE:

1. Make a list of at least one animal for each letter of the alphabet. For a real challenge, try to list at least three animals per letter. Or make an illustrated alphabet book for a beginning reader. Use one animal per page and print the name of each animal beneath the corresponding picture.

2. Make a set of animal flash cards for beginning readers. The animal's picture should be on one side of the card and its name on the other.

3. Draw or paint a picture to show a scene that may have occurred at the tea party. Cut the picture into jigsaw puzzle pieces, put the pieces in an envelope, and give your puzzle to a friend to put together.

4. Write a letter to a friend describing this book and telling why you did or did not like it.

BOOK TITLE:

Mirette On The High Wire

AUTHOR: Emily Arnold McCully
ILLUSTRATOR: Emily Arnold McCully
PUBLISHER: G.P. Putnam

SYNOPSIS:

A young girl's dreams come true as she learns the secrets of wire walking from the Great Bellini. In teaching Mirette the skills she needs to be successful, the master realizes the tremendous faith she has placed in him. As they perform together high above the crowd, he is forced to put aside his own fears and believe in the confidence and excitement of his new protegée.

POINTS TO PONDER:

1. What convinced Bellini that Mirette was indeed serious about learning to wire walk?

2. What do you think Mirette means when she tells Bellini that he must "make it (his fear) leave"?

3. What mood or feeling do the illustrations create? Explain.

4. Describe the disappointment Mirette was feeling in the middle of the story. Compare her situation to one of your own experiences involving disappointment.

5. Explain how Mirette helps the Great Bellini to find courage once again.

PROJECTS TO PURSUE:

1. Draw a line on the ground using chalk. Create your own wire walking routine and practice your moves to get them smooth and graceful. Remember to "never let your eyes stray"!

2. Research a famous circus performer. Note how this person began his or her career and identify the special tricks and daring stunts which made him or her famous. Design a poster or some other colorful display to demonstrate what you learned.

3. Write a list of the dreams you hope to accomplish during your lifetime. Rank them in order of importance to you. Write detailed plans of action telling how you will go about making your top three dreams a reality. Revise your list as needed and refer to it often to help keep your goals in sight.

**BOOK TITLE:**

The Mysterious Tadpole

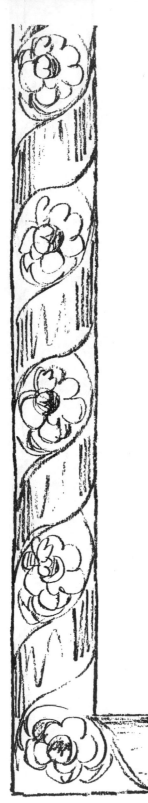

AUTHOR: Steven Kellogg
ILLUSTRATOR: Steven Kellogg
PUBLISHER: Dial Books for Young Readers

## SYNOPSIS:

Uncle McAllister, who lives in Scotland, sends Louis unusual gifts for his nature collection. For Louis's birthday, his uncle sends him a tadpole named Alphonse. As the tadpole outgrows the sink, the bathtub, and the school swimming pool, it becomes obvious that this is no ordinary tadpole. This story chronicles the adventures of Louis and his tadpole looking for a new home in the city.

POINTS TO PONDER:

1. Why would this be considered a fantasy story?

2. Describe how the illustrations in this book can almost tell the story without any words.

3. Why do you think Alphonse looks happy in all of the illustrations? How do the other people in the story look?

4. What kind of person do you think Uncle McAllister is? What did Louis's parents think of him?

5. Do you think a creature the size of the supposed Loch Ness monster (75 feet) could have once been a tadpole?

PROJECTS TO PURSUE:

1. The illustrations in *The Mysterious Tadpole* are very detailed. Choose any page to study and describe in detail. Use that illustration as the basis of an original story of your own.

2. Research the Loch Ness monster. Write a summary of your information complete with sketches showing how you think the Loch Ness monster might look.

3. Share ideas and create a group story for the gift that Uncle McAllister gives Louis at the end of this book. Type or print your text, and add detailed illustrations to create another fantasy story book.

BOOK TITLE:

Odds 'n' Ends
Alvy

AUTHOR: John Frank
ILLUSTRATOR: G. Brian Karas
PUBLISHER: Four Winds Press

SYNOPSIS:

Alvy Flynn is a most unusual character because he is continuously tapping, tugging, twisting, and transforming odds and ends into all kinds of unusual inventions.

POINTS TO PONDER:

1. What is the significance of the title of this story?

2. How did the other kids feel about Alvy Flynn as a friend and classmate? How do you know?

3 How does the illustrator use pictures and varied print size/shape/spacing to enhance the storyline? Give specific examples to support your ideas.

4. Can you find many examples of similes and onomatopoeia in the story? If so, write them down or be ready to point them out to others.

5 Why do you think author John Frank wrote this story?

 **PROJECTS TO PURSUE:**

1. With a group of friends, collect pieces of junk (paper, sequins, ribbons, buttons, stamps, stickers, etc.) and put them in an "odds 'n' ends" box. Use these items to create a piece of original junk art.

2. Create a desk design for your classroom that is an unusual shape, color, design, or texture and that is reflective of your special interests.

3. Browse through a number of magazines and newspapers looking for words written in varied sizes, shapes, and colors. Cut these out and arrange them in a free verse form on a piece of plain paper.

BOOK TITLE: *Oh, The Places You'll Go!*

AUTHOR: Dr. Seuss
ILLUSTRATOR: Dr. Seuss
PUBLISHER: Random House

SYNOPSIS:

This book represents a brief "graduation speech" by Dr. Seuss that provides the reader with humorous verse and pictures addressing the Great Balancing Act of life itself and the potential for success that lies within each of us.

POINTS TO PONDER:

1. Summarize the primary message of this book.

2. This story has been called a "graduation" speech. Who do you think is graduating and what advice are they given by Dr. Seuss?

3. How does Dr. Seuss use humor, rhyme, and language to convey his colorful ideas to the reader?

4. How would you describe the graphics in this book?

5. Why do you think Dr. Seuss is such a popular author with both children and adults?

PROJECTS TO PURSUE:

1. Design a special award that captures the humor and imagination of the great Dr. Seuss.

2. Plan a "Dr. Seuss Celebration" for your classroom or school. Have students come dressed as Dr. Seuss characters, read Dr. Seuss books, draw Dr. Seuss pictures, and play Dr. Seuss games.

3. Draw a series of pictures to show how people in your class like to "un-slump" themselves when they encounter "bang-ups" and "hang-ups."

BOOK TITLE:

Only Opal
(The Diary Of A Young Girl)

AUTHOR: Jane Boulton
ILLUSTRATOR: Barbara Cooney
PUBLISHER: Philomel Books

SYNOPSIS:

Opal Whiteley, who was adopted by an Oregon family, found herself uprooted nineteen times as her family moved from one lumber camp to another. In this book, she finds time to write about her hard life each afternoon. The reader is thus able to share her most intimate thoughts.

POINTS TO PONDER:

1. How does Opal get along with her adoptive parents and family?

2. Describe a typical day for Opal during these years. How is her typical day both like and unlike a typical day in your life?

3. Who was Michael Raphael and what part did he play in Opal's life?

4. Why do you think Opal was so compulsive about keeping a daily diary?

5. Barbara Cooney's illustrations in this book are said to be "beautifully gentle paintings." Why would they be described in this way?

PROJECTS TO PURSUE:

1. Maintain a personal diary for a week of your life. Try to record (in detail) your observations, experiences, feelings, and emotions.

2. Research to find out more about lumber camps and logging as a way of life for families in the early 1900s. Prepare a short "chalk-talk" on this topic to share with the class. A chalk-talk involves drawing a special picture, diagram, or outline on the chalkboard as you give the facts of your report. You should draw in one detail for each fact until you have completed an illustration that is related in some way to the theme of your report.

3. Collect one or more poems by Elizabeth Barrett Browning. Choose one to read aloud to the class.

4. Create a dance or series of creative movements to depict the feelings Opal might have experienced during these hard times.

BOOK TITLE: *The Quilt Story*

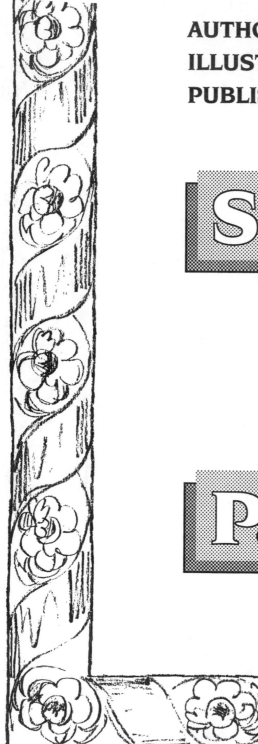

AUTHOR: Tony Johnston
ILLUSTRATOR: Tomie de Paola
PUBLISHER: Putnam

SYNOPSIS:

A mother stitches her daughter Abigail's name on a special quilt. The quilt travels with the family and is put away in the attic where it is adopted by mice, a raccoon, and a cat. It is later found by another little girl, repaired by her mother, and once again used and loved.

POINTS TO PONDER:

1. Why was this quilt made? Why was the name which was sewn on the quilt important to the story?

2. Why did the mother who made the quilt hum as she stitched on the quilt? Why did the second mother resew the quilt for her own daughter?

3. What possession do you remember from your childhood that made you feel better (examples: blanket, teddy bear, stuffed pillow, etc.)? Why was this item so special?

4. How would you retell this story to someone without the book?

5. What message do you think the author is trying to convey through this story?

PROJECTS TO PURSUE:

1. Make a crazy quilt. Use scrap pieces of fabric and design patchwork squares to be sewn together as a group patchwork quilt. Use the quilt as a wall hanging, or present it to a needy family.

2. Make geometrical designs using triangles, squares, rectangles, and circles of colored paper to make quilt piece designs which illustrate mathematical patterns. Display your quilt patterns on a class bulletin board.

3. Research the history of quilts and the stories that they tell. Share the stories with one another and with other classes.

4. Using the same set of characters and the same setting, give this story a different sequence of events and/or a different ending.

BOOK TITLE: *The Rag Coat*

AUTHOR: Lauren Mills
ILLUSTRATOR: Lauren Mills
PUBLISHER: Little, Brown & Co.

SYNOPSIS:

When Minna needs a winter coat to go to school, the Quilting Mothers make her a coat from scraps of material that tell stories of the scraps' previous owners. Although her classmates make fun of her when she wears her coat to school, Minna remembers her Papa's words and appreciates the memories.

POINTS TO PONDER:

1. Use the text and illustrations to identify possible times and places for this story to have taken place.

2. Imagine not being able to go to school. What would your reaction be?

3. Describe the character of Papa.

4. The illustrations in this book are soft, sensitive watercolors. Why do they fit so well with the story?

5. Think about the reactions of Minna's classmates. What would you have done had you been in Minna's place?

PROJECTS TO PURSUE:

1. Use references to research the Appalachian region of the United States. Outline the region on a map and share information about the history and life in this region. What kinds of changes are taking place in this region? How has coal mining played an important role in the area? Name some famous people who were born in Appalachia.

2. Find art and craft books that give directions for making Appalachian crafts. Try your hand at weaving, doll making, wood carving, or quilt making. Also share traditional Appalachian music and stories.

3. Use watercolors or pastel chalks on wet paper to create an additional illustration for one scene or event in the story. Try to capture the mood of the story with the use of the color and imagery.

4. Create a video script to present *The Rag Coat* to a television audience. Include notes for suggested photography shots to accompany the script.

BOOK TITLE: *The Relatives Came*

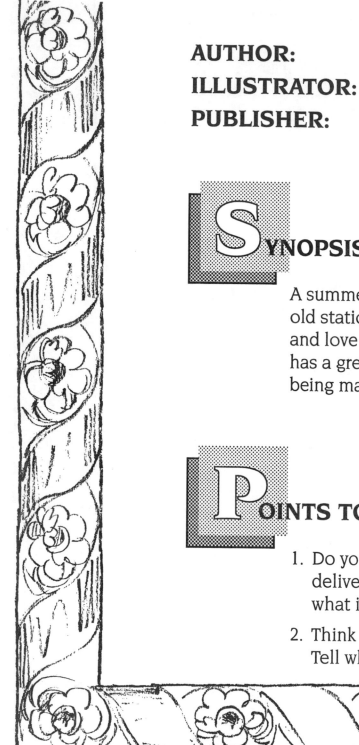

AUTHOR: Cynthia Rylant
ILLUSTRATOR: Stephen Gammell
PUBLISHER: Bradbury Press

SYNOPSIS:

A summer visit from relatives who arrive in a big old station wagon with baskets of food, laughter, and love sets the scene for this story. Everyone has a great time, and the story ends with plans being made for next year's summer reunion.

POINTS TO PONDER:

1. Do you think the author was trying to deliver a message with this story? If so, what is the message?

2. Think of a new name for this story. Tell why you like this name.

3. In which library do you think this book would be most popular?
    (a) a middle school media center
    (b) a summer camp library
    (c) a public library for people of all ages
    (d) a cruise ship library
  Give reasons for your answer.

4. Which do you think contributes the most to this book's success? Why?
    (a) the illustrations
    (b) the plot
    (c) the author's writing style

PROJECTS TO PURSUE:

1. Write a review of *The Relatives Came* suitable for your local newspaper.

2. Design a menu and entertainment guide for a farewell picnic to celebrate the relatives' visit.

3. Write a creative story about an adventure that might have occurred during the relatives' trip home.

4. Write a character sketch of one of your favorite relatives. Emphasize the character traits that make this particular relative special to you.

BOOK TITLE:

The Runaway Bunny

AUTHOR: Margaret Wise Brown
ILLUSTRATOR: Clement Hurd
PUBLISHER: Harper & Row

SYNOPSIS:

In this delightful story, a bunny tells his mother that he will run away, and she responds by indicating how she will catch him if he does.

POINTS TO PONDER:

1. Describe the different arguments for running away that the bunny gives to his mother. How does she respond to each one?

2. Why do you think the author chose a bunny to portray her ideas rather than another animal such as a chipmunk, a dog, a bear, or an elephant?

3. Do you think the bunny was serious about running away from home, or do you think he was teasing his mother about the possibility? Have you ever threatened to run away from home without intending to do so? Explain.

4. List the possible dangers that the bunny might encounter if running away from home. What dangers might you encounter if you ran away from home? Are there any similarities?

5. What advice would you give to a friend who was planning to run away from home?

PROJECTS TO PURSUE:

1. Research to find out what help and resources are available in your community for kids who run away from home.

2. Compose a poem, jingle, or rap that expresses how you feel about running away from home. Include reasons that support your opinion.

3. Design a "door hanger" for your room to maintain your privacy from family intruders when you are angry or upset about something. Some messages that others have used include:

PLEASE DO NOT DISTURB AS I AM DISTURBED ENOUGH!

or

I'M NOT DEAF, I'M JUST IGNORING YOU FOR NOW!

BOOK TITLE:

Sea Swan

AUTHOR: Kathryn Lasky
ILLUSTRATOR: Catherine Stock
PUBLISHER: Macmillan

SYNOPSIS:

A visit from Mrs. Swan's grandchildren causes her to remember the good times of her youth and brings back memories of goals and desires that were never accomplished. These thoughts inspire her to make some changes in her life that help her to gain a new sense of purpose and self-respect.

POINTS TO PONDER:

1. Choose several adjectives to describe the mood of this story. Explain why you selected each word.

2. How do you think Mrs. Swan's children (the parents of her grandchildren) feel about their mother's life changes? How could they help her achieve her goals?

3. Is there a lesson about life to be learned from this story? If so, what is it?

4. Pretend that you are one of Mrs. Swan's grandchildren. What gift would you give her for her next birthday?

ROJECTS TO PURSUE:

1. Interview an elderly person you know. Find out if this person feels that his or her goals were achieved and if those goals were worthy of working toward.

2. Create a new ending for this story based on a different set of goals Mrs. Swan may have had.

3. Make a list of things you want to do as an adult and evaluate each one as a possibility, a probability, or an impossibility.

4. Order each item on your list according to its importance to your hopes and dreams for the future. For the top item on your list, write three things you can do now to help you achieve this goal.

BOOK TITLE:

The Secret In The Matchbox

AUTHOR: Val Willis
ILLUSTRATOR: John Shelley
PUBLISHER: Farrar, Straus, Giroux

SYNOPSIS:

Bobby Bell has a secret hidden in a matchbox. No one, particularly his teacher Miss Potts, wants to know his secret. When he opens the matchbox, a small dragon appears before his classmates. It is not until the dragon grows as big as a bear and breathes fire that it is acknowledged by Miss Potts. Once this happens, Bobby Bell returns it to his matchbox.

POINTS TO PONDER:

1. How did you feel when no one wanted to see what was in the matchbox?

2. What is the significance of Miss Potts's disbelief? What does this indicate about the difference between children and adults?

3. The illustrations are very expressive and detailed. How does this help convey the excitement of this book?

4. How do the picture borders complement as well as enhance the content of each page?

5. Have you ever had a special "show and tell"? What did you bring? Tell about it.

PROJECTS TO PURSUE:

1. Draw a border around the edge of a sheet of drawing paper. Draw something that happens in your classroom inside the large space. In the border, illustrate objects found in your classroom. Display your "framed" class activity pictures.

2. Collect matchboxes of various sizes. Find objects that can fit inside the boxes (toy cars, paper clips, toothpicks, marbles). How many of each object can fit?

3. Write and share stories about your "show and tell" memories. Have a special "show and tell" time scheduled for a class period. Your "secret" must be small enough to fit in a matchbox.

BOOK TITLE:

The Sign Of The Seahorse

AUTHOR: Graeme Base
ILLUSTRATOR: Graeme Base
PUBLISHER: Harry N. Abrams, Inc.

SYNOPSIS:

Bright, colorful illustrations, full of detail and expression, combined with a descriptive and adventurous text take the reader on a journey from the Old Reef to the Great Continental Shelf. The cast of characters includes Pearl and Finneus Trout, Gropmund G. Grouper, the Catfish Gang, and various Fine Young Fish and other Reef-Folk. This is a great adventure story in which good triumps over evil.

POINTS TO PONDER:

1. This is an adventure story. At what points do you find yourself wondering "what will happen next"?

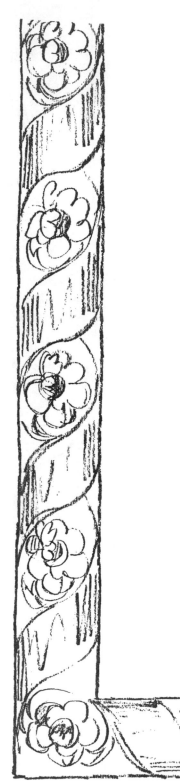

2. There are obvious heroes and villains in this story. Identify them.

3. Why are the illustrations so important in this book?

4. What special features make this a picture book of interest to older readers as well as younger children?

5. How does the poetry format influence the reading of this story? In your opinion, is this a good or bad influence?

6. What is the overall lesson described in this story?

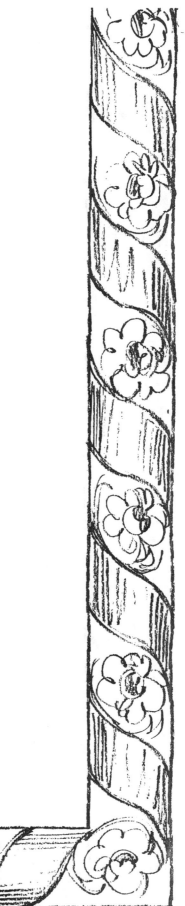

PROJECTS TO PURSUE:

1. Use factual references to define and describe the underwater locations used in this story. Research and share information about ocean reefs, the Great Continental Shelf, mountains of the deep, ocean plains, chasms, crags, and caves.

2. Choose an illustration, a character, or an event from the story to describe in detail. Design a mobile to accompany your description.

3. Write a letter to a friend retelling or summarizing this story. Be sure to include what you believe is the message of the story.

4. Prepare a brief statement appropriate to leave on the author's answering machine. You may tell what you liked, what you disliked, and even offer suggestions for improvements in your message.

BOOK TITLE: *The Sign Painter's Dream*

AUTHOR: Roger Roth

ILLUSTRATOR: Roger Roth

PUBLISHER: Crown Publishers, Inc.

SYNOPSIS:

Clarence, the sign painter, is bored with his life. The only enjoyment he gets now is from reading about Revolutionary War heroes who performed wonderful and exciting deeds. When Clarence is asked to paint a magnificent sign for free, he becomes insulted and refuses to do so until something changes his mind.

POINTS TO PONDER:

1. Why is Clarence always in a bad mood and what does he do about it?

2. What favor is Clarence asked to perform by the small, gray-haired woman and how does he react to this request?

3. What finally persuades Clarence to accommodate the apple lady's appeal for help?

4. How would you describe the illustrations in this story?

5. What do you think is the significance of the title of this book? What makes you think as you do?

PROJECTS TO PURSUE:

1. Pretend you are a famous sign painter like Clarence. Paint a glorious and magnificent sign that you would like to see in your community.

2. Add extra lines to this rhyme from the story: "A *hero is he who helps people for free. A slimeball, you see, will charge them a fee.*"

3. Locate an apple recipe from a cookbook and prepare it as an "apple treat" for the class.

4. Write a short skit or play with one of the following titles:
   "A *Sign of the Times*"
   "*The Boy/Girl Who Upset the Apple Cart*"
   "*It Was the Apple of My Eye*"
   "*The Apple Polisher*"

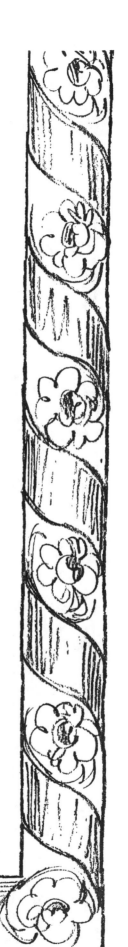

BOOK TITLE:

Socrates And The Three Little Pigs

AUTHOR: Tuyosi Mori
ILLUSTRATOR: Mitsumasa Anno
PUBLISHER: Philomel Books

SYNOPSIS:

Although this book can be enjoyed just for its story and pictures, *Socrates and the Three Little Pigs* actually has much more to offer. It is really an illustrated book about mathematical permutations and combinations. The story of Socrates and the three little pigs can be condensed into a simply phrased question: "In how many ways can 3 pigs be arranged among 5 houses?" Socrates is faced with many difficulties in determining the answer as there is a great deal of important information that is not stated but that can be inferred by the mathematical reader.

POINTS TO PONDER:

1. What do you find is the most unusual thing about this book? Explain.

2. How would you describe the characterization, plot, and setting of this story?

3. What is the significance of the title of this book?

4. How does this story compare with other versions of *The Three Little Pigs* which you may have heard or read? .

5. Would you consider this book to be more of a parody or a satire? Give reasons to support your answer.

PROJECTS TO PURSUE:

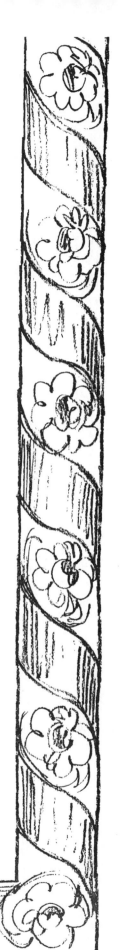

1. Research to find out something about the life and philosophy of Socrates. Write a report about him.

2. Define the word "philosophy." Write your philosophy of life using a metaphor or simile to express your ideas. Two samples are given below.

> *Life is like an elevator because it has so many ups and downs.*
>
> *Life is like a maze. It teases you with so many roads to choose from, but so many of them lead to a dead end.*

3. Choose another popular fairy tale or fable and try to rewrite it with a mathematical twist.

OOK TITLE:

AUTHOR: Arnold Adoff
ILLUSTRATOR: Steve Kuzma
PUBLISHER: J. B. Lippincott

YNOPSIS:

In this collection of carefully structured, yet free-moving, poems the reader moves from sport to sport learning what it means to be an athlete. Both the words and the illustrations depict the rhythmic, musical evocation of both movement and thought.

POINTS TO PONDER:

1. List the sports reflected in this collection of poems.

2. How do both the poet and the illustrator use space and line to depict the various sports?

3. What are the different sports-related messages conveyed to the reader through the language of these poems?

4. What is your definition of an athlete? What are some qualities that you believe make a successful athlete?

5. Why do you think the illustrator limited his use of color in the illustrations?

PROJECTS TO PURSUE:

1. Pretend that you just broke a world's record in a sport of your choice. Write a spectacular news story recounting your glorious moment of triumph.

2. Create a commemorative stamp displaying a sport of your choice.

3. Design a billboard promoting sportsmanship for students of your age group. Include a slogan that will be easily remembered.

4. Work in groups to develop a cheer that encourages sportsmanship and teamwork. Perform your cheers for one another.

BOOK TITLE: *The Story Of May*

AUTHOR: Mordicai Gerstein
ILLUSTRATOR: Mordicai Gerstein
PUBLISHER: Harper Collins

SYNOPSIS:

This is a story about the month of May who lives with her mother, April. However, she has never met her father, December, who lives in the cold—far across the year. This special story of family love is set in the richness of the passing seasons where each month has a special task or purpose for its existence.

POINTS TO PONDER:

1. Why is this book considered to be an allegory?

2. Who are the main characters in the story? What is the plot of the story?

3. What contribution does each month make to May's search for her father?

4. Do you like the way the story ended? Why or why not?

5. Which month represents your favorite individual? Give reasons to support your answer.

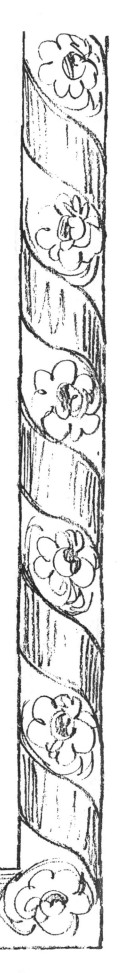

PROJECTS TO PURSUE:

1. Browse through the calendars offered in a popular bookstore. Explain how these calendars are a form of art.

2. Pretend that you are a discarded calendar at the end of the year. Write a journal or diary entry telling how you feel and what happens to you after December 31.

3. Create a short play using selected months of the year as the main characters. Build your play around a universal theme.

4. Invent a 13th month of the year. Give it a name and tell where it would fit within the existing months. Describe what the weather would typically be like during this new month and tell of any holidays that would occur in it as well.

BOOK TITLE: *Strega Nona*

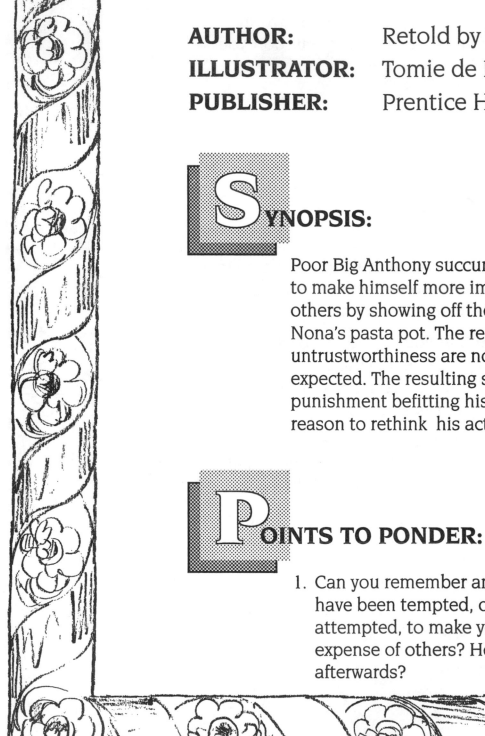

AUTHOR: Retold by Tomie de Paola
ILLUSTRATOR: Tomie de Paola
PUBLISHER: Prentice Hall

SYNOPSIS:

Poor Big Anthony succumbs to the temptation to make himself more important in the eyes of others by showing off the magic of Strega Nona's pasta pot. The results of his untrustworthiness are not at all what he expected. The resulting stomachache and punishment befitting his misdeed give him reason to rethink his actions.

POINTS TO PONDER:

1. Can you remember an occasion when you have been tempted, or have actually attempted, to make yourself important at the expense of others? How did you feel afterwards?

2. If you had a magic pot and you could use it only three times before the magic left it, what would you cook in it, and how would you share the food cooked?

3. Do you think Big Anthony's behavior was permanently changed by this experience with Strega Nona? If so, how and to what extent?

PROJECTS TO PURSUE:

1. Tomie de Paola is a talented and well-known author and illustrator. Find out something about his life and works. Locate other books that have been both written and illustrated by him. Try to identify similarities and differences in his styles of writing and illustrating. Can you note special changes in books that were produced at different dates in his life?

2. Devise a unique pasta recipe that might have been appropriate for pasta from the magic pot.

3. Research the history of pasta. You may be surprised to learn that, contrary to popular opinion, pasta did not originate in Italy!

4. Create a cartoon or comic strip showing Big Anthony and Strega Nona engaged in a conversation that might have occurred following the conclusion of the story.

BOOK TITLE: # Sylvester And The Magic Pebble

AUTHOR: William Steig
ILLUSTRATOR: William Steig
PUBLISHER: Simon & Schuster

SYNOPSIS:

Sylvester collects pebbles. One day he finds a magic pebble that makes wishes come true. Sylvester is very happy about his pebble until he accidentally wishes to be a rock. After returning to his normal self, Sylvester finds that he has learned an important lesson about life.

POINTS TO PONDER:

1. What would you wish for if you could have any wish in the world granted?

2. What type of motivation caused Sylvester to get into trouble?

3. Why do you think the author chose to make all of the characters animals?

4. What did Mr. and Mrs. Duncan do to try to find their son? How did they try to go on with their life?

5. What lesson do you think Sylvester learned from this experience?

6. Do you think the Duncans ever took the rock out of the iron safe? Would you?

PROJECTS TO PURSUE:

1. Retell the story in your own words. List and categorize the adjectives needed to make the story interesting without the benefit of pictures.

2. Rewrite the story using people as the characters instead of animals.

3. Construct a survey to find the top five wishes among the people in your class.

4. For fun, jot down a list of "wishes" heard in school and at home for a week. Compare and contrast student lists.

BOOK TITLE: *Tikki Tikki Tembo*

AUTHOR: Arlene Mosel
ILLUSTRATOR: Blair Lent
PUBLISHER: Holt

SYNOPSIS:

The Chinese tradition of giving first sons long names is changed when a little boy with a long name almost drowns. Tikki Tikki Tembo – No Sa Rembo – Chari Bari Ruchi – Pip Peri Pembo almost loses his life in the well because his name takes too long to say. Chang, the second son, is saved quickly.

POINTS TO PONDER:

1. How would you feel about being called "little or nothing" instead of "the most wonderful thing in the whole wide world"? What do you think this difference in names has to do with the main point of the story?

2. Compare the mother's reactions when told about her two sons falling into the well. What was the reaction of the Old Man with the Ladder?

3. Discuss the significance of the full-page illustrations used in this story.

4. What was Tikki Tikki Tembo – No Sa Rembo – Chari Bari Ruchi – Pip Peri Pembo renamed? Discuss some other possibilities.

PROJECTS TO PURSUE:

1. Make up names for other Chinese characters. How many ten-word names can you create that have a musical or rhythmic quality? Write each name, give each an English meaning, and illustrate a character for each.

2. Use references to find the history and significance of Chinese traditions (such as the use of dragons, names of parade characters, or why different years are named after animals, etc.). Share your reports.

3. Find examples of Chinese writing. Practice writing the Chinese alphabet. Try writing your name in Chinese. Use pen and ink for more authentic-looking writing.

BOOK TITLE: *Tree Of Cranes*

AUTHOR: Allen Say
ILLUSTRATOR: Allen Say
PUBLISHER: Houghton Mifflin

SYNOPSIS:

While paying the price for a cold caught at a forbidden pond, a little boy in Japan is introduced to his mother's favorite Christmas traditions from her childhood in America. This is the story of a boy's memory of a peaceful and quiet first Christmas.

POINTS TO PONDER:

1. How does the little boy know he will get into trouble? When does he know that his mother knows where he has been?

2. The boy does not argue with the consequences of his actions. What were the consequences and how do you think the boy felt about each one? Have you ever had similar feelings?

3. How do you view Christmas? In what ways are your perceptions of Christmas similar to and different from those of the boy and his mother? Explain.

4. How well do you think the watercolor pictures illustrate this story? Why?

PROJECTS TO PURSUE:

1. The Japanese mother made paper cranes to decorate the small pine tree. Find an instruction book on origami and make peace cranes and other small ornaments. Hang these from mobiles to decorate your classroom. Research the history of origami.

2. Use references to find information on Japanese gardens. Create a Japanese garden in pictures, collage, or peep-box format.

3. The boy wished for and received a special Japanese kite. Make decorative kites of your own using tissue paper, dowel sticks, and string.

4. Research Japanese holidays and share your findings with the group.

BOOK TITLE:

The True Story Of The 3 Little Pigs

AUTHOR: A. Wolf As Told To Jon Scieszka
ILLUSTRATOR: Lane Smith
PUBLISHER: Viking Kestrel

SYNOPSIS:

This is a story of the three little pigs told from the perspective of the big bad wolf.

POINTS TO PONDER:

1. What does Jon Scieszka add to the telling of this story by pretending that the true author is A. Wolf? Do you think he is successful?

2. How does this book introduce the concept of "point of view," so important in the teaching of literature?

3. How do the illustrations enhance the reading of the story? Give examples to support your position.

4. Compare and contrast this book with the original version of *The Three Little Pigs*. Which do you think is the "real" story? Why?

5. Who was the villain in this version? Explain your answer.

PROJECTS TO PURSUE:

1. Act out this story and the original story of *The Three Little Pigs* for another class or group of students. Follow these skits with a group discussion of which version represents the "real" story.

2. Choose another popular fairy tale and rewrite it from a different perspective.

3. Design a bookmark for a local library or bookstore to promote the sale or reading of this book.

4. Create a new character for this story to be known as the "fourth little pig." Work your character into the story's plot in such a way that the sequence of events and outcome are changed.

BOOK TITLE: *The Velveteen Rabbit*

AUTHOR: Margery Williams
ILLUSTRATOR: David Jorgensen
PUBLISHER: Alfred A. Knopf, Inc.

SYNOPSIS:

This popular children's classic is a story about a toy rabbit, made out of velveteen, and his love for the boy who owned him. The relationship of the boy and the rabbit is very special, but it changes over time due to circumstances beyond their control.

(Note: *This book will require more than one reading period and should be planned for use accordingly.*)

POINTS TO PONDER:

1. What is the setting of this story and who are the major characters? How do the illustrations enhance the setting and the characters?

2. What type of relationship does the Velveteen Rabbit have with his owner, and how does it change as the boy grows older?

3. How do the other rabbits feel about the Velveteen Rabbit when they first meet him? Why?

4. How would you describe Skin Horse, and how does he influence the outcome of this story?

5. What does it mean to be real in this story?

PROJECTS TO PURSUE:

1. Create a web to show the many different feelings that are depicted in this story. Cite words, phrases, and sentences from the story to support the feeling words listed as part of your web.

2. Write a story about a teddy bear who is discarded by a young teenager who feels he or she has outgrown stuffed toys.

3. Hold a white elephant sale for used games, toys, and stuffed animals that belong to students in your class. Label each item for sale with a small tag that gives a brief history of the object.

BOOK TITLE:

The Very Hungry Caterpillar

AUTHOR: Eric Carle
ILLUSTRATOR: Eric Carle
PUBLISHER: Collins World

SYNOPSIS:

The story tells about the life of a caterpillar from a little egg on a leaf to a beautiful butterfly. Illustrations play a very important part in describing what the caterpillar ate over the course of his journey.

POINTS TO PONDER:

1. How do the illustrations and the holes in the drawings affect the reader? Do you want to touch where the holes are placed? Why do you think this might be important for younger readers?

2. How good are your memory skills? How many times do you need to look at the book to make a list of what the caterpillar ate?

3. Do you think a caterpillar really eats through a pickle, a lollipop, and the other foods listed as his Saturday meal?

4. Do you think this author is effective at presenting science and math skills to young children? How?

5. Is there something else you want the caterpillar to eat or do?

PROJECTS TO PURSUE:

1. Research and study the life cycle of a butterfly. Report and display your findings with the use of dioramas and charts.

2. Work in a group to make tissue-paper collages of things in nature.

3. Make various food group items with holes in them. String them to be used by a group of younger students for counting and categorizing activities.

BOOK TITLE: *The Wall*

AUTHOR: Eve Bunting
ILLUSTRATOR: Ronald Himler
PUBLISHER: Clarion Books

SYNOPSIS:

This is the story of a father and his young son who have come to the Vietnam Veterans' Memorial to find the name of the grandfather the little boy never knew. They experience feelings of both pride and sadness as they locate Grandpa's name on the wall.

POINTS TO PONDER:

1. What is the purpose of the Vietnam Memorial, and where is it located?

2. What makes this story so moving and poignant?

3. What kind of an impact do the illustrations have on the emotions of the reader?

4. What kinds of things do the father and son see and do at the Vietnam Memorial?

5. Why did the author choose not to give either the son or the father a name? Does this make a difference to the reader? Explain your response.

PROJECTS TO PURSUE:

1. Research to find out about the history and significance of war memorials. Report your findings in some visual way to the class.

2. Compare and contrast the Berlin Wall with the Vietnam Memorial. How are they alike, and how are they different?

3. Design a "wall memorial" to commemorate a past or present historical event. Where is it located? What does it look like? Who does it attract? Why is it important?

BOOK TITLE: The Wednesday Surprise

AUTHOR: Eve Bunting
ILLUSTRATOR: Donald Carrick
PUBLISHER: Clarion Books

SYNOPSIS:

Every Wednesday night, Anna spends precious time with her Grandma at home, sharing picture books and reading stories. There is a special purpose for these meetings: Anna's father finds that out in the "birthday surprise of his life."

POINTS TO PONDER:

1. What type of person is Anna? How do you know this?

2. Why would Anna take pleasure in spending so much time with her grandma?

3. What books from your childhood would you have chosen to read and share with Grandma?

4. Why is it that Grandma has never learned to read until now? What circumstances might have caused this situation?

5. What other experiences can different generations share with one another to enrich all of their lives? Be specific in your responses.

PROJECTS TO PURSUE:

1. Prepare a list of picture book titles that would be appropriate for sharing with older people who are learning how to read better, who are in nursing homes and are unable to read, or who have never had the opportunity to encounter picture books as a child.

2. Develop a plan for improving the literacy of adults in your community. What would you do and how would you do it?

3. How and why has reading for pleasure become an "endangered species" in today's society? Design a poster urging people of your age to develop habits leading to the lifelong pleasure of reading.

BOOK TITLE: *Whale Is Stuck*

AUTHOR: Karen Hayles
ILLUSTRATOR: Charles Fuge
PUBLISHER: Simon & Schuster

SYNOPSIS:

Whale loved to splash in and out of the open sea, and Fish always swam alongside him. One day, Whale lands on an ice floe and gets stuck. His friends Walrus, the Dolphins and Porpoises, Sea Birds, Seals, Polar Bears, and even Narwhal try to get him off of the ice. Only time and nature helped get Whale back into the water.

POINTS TO PONDER:

1. Whale had many friends who tried to help him. Were they successful? Did Whale always appreciate their efforts?

2. Were Whale and Fish friends? Support your answer with specific information from the text and illustrations.

3. This is a story about friendship. Is there another message concerning the whale?

4. The eyes of the characters in the story's illustrations are very expressive. What do you "see" when you look into their eyes?

5. Some words in the text are printed in bold type. What purpose does this bold type serve?

6. What do you think Fish was thinking when Whale didn't splash back into the ocean?

PROJECTS TO PURSUE:

1. Research the Arctic sea life written about in the story: whale, walrus, dolphin, porpoise, seal, sea bird, polar bear, narwhal. Make lists of characteristics of these animals. Compare and contrast the characteristics.

2. Create a cartoon strip telling what the different sea life creatures are saying to each other while helping get Whale back into the water. Don't forget to give the animals expressive faces comparable to the illustrations in the book.

3. Find reference materials and illustrations of Arctic regions. Discover what makes an ice floe. Design a mural with Arctic scenery and animals.

BOOK TITLE:

Wilfrid Gordon McDonald Partridge

AUTHOR: Mem Fox
ILLUSTRATOR: Julie Vivas
PUBLISHER: Kane/Miller

SYNOPSIS:

This book chronicles a small boy's efforts to help an elderly friend regain her lost memory. As he attempts to find the meaning of "memory," Wilfrid Gordon McDonald Partridge interacts with other older friends and translates the wisdom gained from them into real items to be shared with Miss Nancy Selison Delacourt Cooper. The items do indeed help his friend recall happy times and fond memories.

POINTS TO PONDER:

1. What is the central message of this story?

2. How do the illustrator's graphic interpretations of the conversations between the young boy and his elderly friends add to the power of this book?

3. What age group do you think this story would most appeal to?

4. Do you think many boys or girls of Wilfrid McDonald McPartridge's age would be as interested in older people as he was?

5. How do you think author Mem Fox's Australian background influenced her choice of items to be included in the "treasure basket"?

PROJECTS TO PURSUE:

1. Outline a project that you could personally plan and carry out to bring a bit of joy into the life of an elderly person of your acquaintance.

2. Work in groups of two or three to decide on items from your own environment that could be used to fill a "memory" basket for Miss Nancy.

3. Create the script for a puppet play that could be presented to a house-bound group of elderly people to make them laugh. Sketch the puppets needed for the play.

4. Write a cheerful letter or design a "Happy Day" card to mail to someone you know who would benefit from an expression of love or friendship.

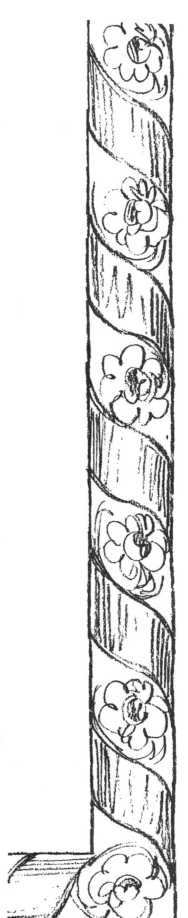